# LOOK OF WONDER

## BY

## BARBARA SAYLES GARNER

For Mairles

© Barbara Sayles Garner

*1988*

ISBN 0948478 35 7

**Acknowledgements**

Some of these poems have appeared in ENVOI, First Time, etc.

ENVOI POETS PUBLICATIONS
PEN FFORDD, NEWPORT, DYFED, SA42 0QT, WALES, U.K.

# CONTENTS

# LOVE

This photograph, so clear ! the nesting swan,
The woman looking on —
Two females: one, this white and shapely form,
Soft-feathered, warm,
Rapt in the acts of love; one, standing by —
Can this be I,
Watching my swan, my sister, unaware
Of hostile camera there,
The sharp incisive camera of today,
Which blurs away
No fold, no wattle, no unfriendly line ?
Can these indeed be mine,
Invisible to my mirror ? Do I see
The cold unexpurgated truth of me,
And as I said, so clear ?
Then, what a wreck is here,
A gross intruder in this sacred place !

  I showed it to my friend; I turned my head.
  'A lovely photograph of you,' he said.
  'I love that look of wonder on your face.'

# CONFLICT

Dido to the haunted wood
From Aeneas turns alone,
Stands unchanging as she stood,
In the moment set as stone;
   And her fingers motionless
   Lie along her carven dress.

But her lover, pulled apart
By ambitions and desires,
Envious of her single heart,
Pleading stumbles, checks, retires:
   Nightly turns from side to side
   On the bed that held his bride.


# FREEDOM

I saw the crippled woman
Walking in the wood:
Envious, the rustling trees
Shook where they stood —

'See how she lifts her roots !'
Whispered their laughter;
'One dropping earth, and one
That drags so slowly after !'

'Ah !' cried the treetop birds:
'What thought goes winging
Past our perching feet ? beyond
Even our singing ?

Up through unbounded air
Soars the ecstatic spirit;
Such lives, empyreal worlds
Claim and inherit.'

# EDEN ORCHARD

Ask me this apricot,
Pray me this plum,
Choose from these cherries —
    Oh come,
This which torments you
Is hunger, is thirst:
Come to your feasting —
    Your first !

Adam, my innocent,
I have decreed
You shall find food
    For your need —
You shall have need
To restore, to replace:
Let me know joy
    From your face !

I, the Creator,
All-perfect, complete,
Cannot renew —
    Cannot eat —
All that surrounds me
Lives out from within;
Pay me your pleasure !
    Begin !


# THE HIDDEN PLACE

'Daring thought, look over the wall,
What do you see ?'
    'I see sprawl
A shape of shadow under a tree.'
'Trees, there are trees ?'
    'Of a sort.'
    'And birds ?'
'Bird and tree are the nearest words;
And shadow sprawled with one bent knee,
    With head aside,
    And arms thrown wide,
Shape of a shadow known to me.'

# THE DINNER

When you sit at my table,
Do I serve you my trouble ?

Do I set in your place
Knives to incise your face ?

Have I poured out this wine
To slake your thirst or mine ?

Hollows deepen as you eat:
Are you my meat ?

     Why then, if this be so,
     Stand up, dear heart, and go.
     Go, though I beg you No.
     Rise, love, and go !


# LEAF AND BUD

I wish you were with me,
You wish I were with you;
We wish we need not be
    Parted: but two

Sure as we were before
Of loving friendship near.
I halt beside your door:
    If you were here !

With me, as any one
Of countless leaves that blow
Down-wind, and then are gone.
    With you, as though

Bud to perfection grown
In axil of that leaf,
Knew, on the branch alone,
    An individual grief.

# PETER

Peter,
Reading by the window,
In the square of lamplight,
The summer evening through;
Over the pages leans
The dark head, motionless;
Timeless, with timeless thought,
The thought intact endures.

With the old wisdom
Pondered by the Aegean
Under the cypress and the pine
Two thousand years before:
Peter, reading
Among the barren chimneys, keeps
An everlasting pace, a turn
Of mind abiding.

Like a ship, anchored
Among the city houses,
Like a full moon in dark skies,
Like a golden island
In a black tideless water,
Shines the uncurtained room
Across the deepening night.

In summer the people walk
Through the stone city gardens
At nightfall, gaze across
The glimmering squares of dusty grass,
The beds of pinks and mignonette;
Home up white pavements pass
With talk and laugh and echoing tread.
In summer the twilight holds
A long remembrance of the sun,
The stars come slowly,
And those who live by time
Turn slowly with the day
To mutual rest.

Peter, reading
Within the shadowing city,
Body and vision rapt
In the gold isle of light,
Neither looks up, nor moves,
Nor hears the people passing
Nor the tick of the clock,
Nor draws the coloured curtain
Between him and the sky.

## ACROSS THE CROWDED ROOM

I am alive to you,
I need not hear nor see,
My body tells me who
Is in this room with me,

All my existence of
Your presence is aware,
And is suffused with love;
And senses, in the air

A heightening of delight:
A gleam across the floor:
A world grown warm and bright
That was not so before.

# REFLECTIONS

Here, from these roses
Deep-drowned, the petals,
Fallen, drifted upward,
Bear cupped above them
Their cool white shadows;
The nymph in the water
Laughs up at her image
Reflected in stone.
We two are visions,
Are phantoms: these lovers
Part, move aside — Farewell !
Our forms dissolve in air !

# FANTASIES

My love, if in your fantasies
I come to you as I would please,
And so relate, and speak, and do,
As would myself, not part of you:
And if in mine you feature so,
Not one I need, but one I know —
Then truth of image holds each heart,
We two have loved, we shall not part.

So we, distinct, yet not alone,
Are both each other's, and our own:
But yet if either one could find
Such image in the other's mind
As made them cry in chill dismay,
'I could not look, nor do, nor say,
As in your dream !' — then, never yet
Have we two loved, or seen, or met.

# MAKING

An old man stood by the road one day;
There came a car and took him away.

'Come,' said the driver, 'Come, get in.'
'No, ah no !' 'Yes, you must get in.'

'I want my book and I want my tea,
And my grandson wants my company.'

'Not your body and not your mind
Nor even your love can stay behind.'

The driver drove him in his car
To the nearby town where most of us are,

And on the pavement where he stood
Lay only a dog carved out of wood.

Sobbing out of the stillness came
A sad little boy who called his name.

He spied the dog and he stooped him down
And took it back to the smaller town.

He stood his treasure beside his bed:
'Granddad made it for me,' he said.

For not the fingers and not the face
Nor even our love can keep their place,

But never chauffeur out of the shade
Shall carry away the toys we made.

# NOTHING

I looked up the hill,
And I saw nothing.
The wind was still
And cold the air.
The stream was ice,
The tree was bare.
No life was there.
I saw it, nothing.

I looked in your eyes,
And I saw nothing.
Neither ill-will
Nor boredom, nothing.
Nothing to stare
At me, nothing.
I saw it, nothing.
Nothing was there.

# THE  STRANGER

The woods are dark and silent now,
Whose leaves in a thousand voices sang
When he and I together
Stood tremulous under their boughs,
And the little Inn at the lane's end
Is empty; knock, and no-one comes.
There's a door nailed up with boards across,
And a notice reading, 'Not for Sale'.

Who was, where is he ? The voice, the eyes,
Were yours, and are: yet I walk with you,
The trees are barren and the Inn decays,
And my heart cries after my lost companion.
If I might only build for him
A tomb ! only learn his name !

# THE OLD WOMAN SPEAKS

My mother was old at fifty,
Her skirts came down to her feet,
When the single girls were virgins,
And carts went by in the street.

I knew where I stood with the Gentry,
I knew where I stood with the Poor,
When hens ran free in the farmyard,
And neighbours knocked on the door.

We spoke of Wars and an Empire,
And the duty of men to die:
Then my husband died, and the Empire:
And what lives on ? Do I ?

Where are the rules and the standards ?
Where is the constant face ?
What should I think or believe in ?
How shall I know my place ?

I shall die in a hospital,
And lie in unhomely clay,
And the Vicar will be a stranger,
And God will have moved away.

# MOVE ON

The house is shut and the master gone away,
The paint flaking, and the glass grey.
    Our time is gone: why stay ?

The ghosts go by that were you and I,
Down the empty street and the night sky.
I hear him pleading, I hear her cry.
    Go with the ghosts, go by.

Why do I wait ? I stand alone
By the darkened house now you are gone.
Where were two are one and one.
    Go then with time, move on.

# THE SERPENT

To and fro
Did I go,
Tall on the tip of my single toe,
Lissoming high and litheing low,
Through Eden greenery, long ago;
In the shade of the Tempting Tree
The pretty young lady danced with me.
The fruit was scented, round, and red,
The Paradise birds sang overhead.
    To and fro
    Did I go,
    Tall on the tip of my single toe,
    Through Eden greenery, long ago.

The Gardener said to us, said he:
'You're not to taste of the Tempting Tree:
Take all the others, but that's for me !
It holds the secret of good and ill —
The secret's mine, and I keep it still !'
The man said, 'Right ! If that's your will !' —
Shouldered his spade and stumped him by.
But pretty young lady wondered Why.
Wondered, wondered, and so did I !
    To and fro
    Did I go,
    Tall on the tip of my single toe,
    Through Eden greenery, long ago.

Alas, the taste of the Tempting Tree !
He turned us out, he did, all three,
The pretty young lady, man, and me !
Low, low,
On my belly I go,
And drag in the dust my single toe.
The fruit was a cheat
That we did eat:
The Gardener keeps his secret still —
They'll never agree on good and ill;
But I must sting and they must kill,
And sorrow and pain we know, we know.
    To and fro
    Did I go,
    Tall on the tip of my single toe,
    Through Eden greenery, long ago.
    Long ago. Long, long ago.
    Long ago.

# CUCKOO

Cuckoo fly home, cuckoo come home,
Cuckoo will call and Spring will come.

I stood at the door, the street was grey:
Cuckoo will call up April and May.

I stood by the shore, the blossoming sea;
A cloud of cuckoos flew in to me,

Out of the South, a shining flight;
Cuckoos come bringing life and light.

Flowering tree sprang out of the sand,
A tide of leaves swept over the land.

Cuckoo come in, cuckoo fly in,
Cuckoo will cry and Spring begin.


# O THE GREEN WILLOW

By green willow water
Where clear streams go straying,
We wandered together.

Among the green islands
The swan stays her motion;
The long weed trails idly
Adrift through the water.
Here would we linger.

I'll make me my bed
In the harsh tufts of heather:
Among the dry forests,
The dry barren uplands,
Forgotten, forgetting,
My home be for ever.
By green willow water
I'll wander no more.

# THE NUTMEG

Your nutmeg, Mother, in this jar,
Is fragrant still, and that is more
Than you and my dear sister are,
Or Father is, gone long before
The two of you, these forty years,
To where I cannot dry his tears.

How crossed, how strange our fortunes are,
That we should die, and others find
Spices in some forgotten jar,
That lacking will or power or mind
Remind them how their loves have been
As firm, sweet-scented, smooth, and clean.


# HELEN'S FUNERAL

The funeral car came down the street,
Shiny, and black, and filled with flowers.
We thought, 'Her turn today, not ours;
We move, we breathe, and life is sweet.'

We stood in groups at Helen's gate
To follow her, when up there ran,
As best he could, a bald old man,
Panting, who called on us to wait,

'Is Mrs. Cotton gone ?' he said —
'Why, only yesterday I heard
A friend dropped in, and said a word,
And found her well, and now she's dead !'

His body shivered, and his face
Was stiff with shock, and white, and cold,
Because he knew that he was old,
And saw in mind his empty place,

And heard our lowered voices say:
'On Helen's funeral day, he came,
And looked and sounded just the same.
And that seems only yesterday.'

# HAMMERSMITH BRIDGE

Away among the chimneys,
Evenings in summer emphasise
The crowded cardboard silhouettes,
Roof, gaswork, spire,
Ripen and render kind
A throng of eager streets, where press
The cramped impatient cars.
Athread the white cold lights
Blaze by the darkening water,
And over Hammersmith Bridge
Come the people crowding,
Jostle and shout and laugh
To the public house or the dance.

How clearly ring, resound,
Footfall and voice !

Up four flights of stairs,
Between the street and the sky,
Enpoised, a world apart,
We keep our fragmentary house.
The stars look straight ahead
With tranced and shining eyes.
The people ponder the stones,
Windows, and one another.
Never look up.

Down by the river-side
We drink at wooden tables, share
The laughter out of doors,
Flies and the moon.
Downstream the single swan
Sails, white in the shadow,
The little boats at mooring dip
Clipped squares of golden light;
While through the wondering twilight rise
The innocent bubbles of sound,
Voices and glass.

Up four flights of stairs
Waits the sloping attic room,
Five shelves with books, one chair,
The bed by the open window.
Far off the passionate stars
Gaze; never downward;
And over Hammersmith Bridge
The people falter,
Dwindle, dream close to sleep,
Musing the stones.

Away among the chimneys
Love waits, and none beside,
Love is, and here are we,
Our love, and he, and I.


## THE FACE


'Gazing in the water,
Love, what do you see ?'
    'I see another face
    Looking up at me.'

'Do you see the green trees,
And do you see the sky ?'
    'In the pool below me
    No reflections lie;

    Tall the weeds are growing
    Through the water clear.
    Shadowless the world is
    That awaits me here.'

'Then you see your own face
Mirrored all alone ?'
    'No. I said, Another face.
    I did not say, My own.'

# PITY COME

Pity come, O Pity come,
Unclench these rocks, set free this sand,
Bind the salt wind, unparch our land,
Renew, restore us, call us home.

A single tear brings pouring rain,
A single touch heals up each wound,
One seed alone greens every ground,
One drop of blood fills every vein.


# THE ROBIN

In the wide eye of the sun
The robin hides, when Spring is gone,
Eggs cracked and fledglings flown:

When the sun climbs to its height,
Strong and swift he takes his flight
Upward, and is lost in light.

Out of sight the summer long,
Silent while the sun is strong —
Clear, sweet, melancholy song

Lost in stillness, and unheard
'Tic-tic' chittering, ratchet-chirred:
Small round out-of-season bird !

In the dwindled golden year,
Brown and russet he'll appear,
Hopping, calling 'I am here,

Watching for the seeded snow
And closely-budded frosts to grow:
Waiting for the world I know.'

# THE YOUNG THRUSH

How young you are, how newly made, how trim,
My girl or boy,
Your baby down all gone, straight-winged and slim !
Ochre this upper breast,
Soft-coloured and soft-feathered, and the rest
Pearl-white, stone-white,
With freckles freshly stippled, brown and bright !
I see you hop a little way: now try
To lift those wings, and fly,
Before the cat comes stalking, or the pie
(Which I can see
Watching you from this tree),
Swoops down: I turn my head, and you are gone —
May you live on,
Next season's nest, this Springtime's lovely song,
Fulfilled, and long !
I look all round; then comes a sudden burst
Of music close at hand, and you are here,
Perched on the roof-ridge, near
As thrushes never perch, once fully grown,
And singing in the heart of day alone,
So pure, so clear,
A thrush's perfect song; is it your first ?
How apt, if this should be,
Sung, as I may imagine it, for me,
Who listen with such love, such depth of joy !


# REMEMBER MY NAME

Herb Robert sprawls about,
May-flower's toppled out:
Jack-by-the-hedge lingers,
Jabs long accusing fingers
Up at the sultry sky.
Each says, 'Now July
Swamps with a surge of green
All my separate life has been,
Drowned in docks, nettles, grass —
Recollect me as you pass:
Here you perceived me, here
In the sparse and springing year
Gave me worship when I came.
Think of my name.'

# IN HALF

Mallow and willow-herb replace
The lovely flowers of May;
I feel I live with half a face,
With self cut half away;

I must live so, and so would you,
If I, not you, were gone —
When life was lived as one of two,
One half of two lives on.

You puzzled me with love denied,
You held our minds apart,
But still my youth was by your side,
Your childhood at my heart.

Come back, although you bring me grief;
Be distant, only be;
And share the frost, the falling leaf,
Though never more with me.


# SPRING

Spring like an inward light
Leaps to our finger-tips,
Brings radiance to the sight
And fullness to the lips:

Instinct and impulse run
To greet the rousing earth,
Share with resurgent sun
Strength, joy, and birth !

Only the stubborn mind
Is locked in ice and frost;
Lamenting, left behind,
All meaning lost —

'Wait, integrate with me !
Find me a reason,
Running with you, to be
Glad for a season !'

# ELD

My father has a forge
By a dark water;
Here he made iron shoes
For his young daughter.

My mother blows the fire
With her heavy breath.
Still in his corner waits
Cold grandsire Death.

My father's name is Eld,
And hers is Accidie.
Now they set out the shoes
Forged there for me:

'Grandchild, hurry home !
Come soon, my daughter !
Tread in our iron shoes
This unsounded water !'

Each in the lonely dark
Stays for my answer:
'Long, long, your shoes await
Pilgrim and dancer.'


# TO A SILENT YOUNG LADY

Come, Fiorella, come,
Call the song-bird to the sky.
Earth is all music: why
Should these curving lips be dumb,
When the curved and slender moon,
Sounding like a hollow shell
        With beckoned seas,
        Brings harmonies
To listening shores in surge and swell ?
Hark, Fiorella, hark,
Lovers calling through the dark
        In sweet accord ! my dear,
Be eloquent of life, proclaim your presence here !
Rouse with the daylight, prove
Kinship with the singing bird;
Break your silence with a word,
        Make that word a word of love.

# ON SHOW

'Oh Mother, see these captive calves
Between the wall and door !
How strange these helpless prisoned hens
I have not seen before !

The pictures in my story-book
Tell me they live outside;
Why are they drawn in cobbled yards,
Or meadows green and wide ?

I never see them in the fields
Where food for me is grown,
When from the windows of our car
I look out all alone.'

    'They live, my child ! in little crates,
    Safe from the open sky !
    They miss their free and natural lives
    No more than you or I.

    Secure they are and fortunate:
    They feel no cold nor wet:
    They need no brains, nor ears, nor eyes,
    Whose every need is met.

    Come home now to our top-floor flat,
    And watch the silver screen,
    And we'll forget who played outside
    Where summer fields were green.'

# THE OLD CANAL

The weeds along the current lie,
The tangled leaf locks out the sky,
And weeping ash and willow lean
Where water curls the reeds between,

Oozes, and slips, and eddies slow
Where moss and cress and lichen grow,
Where grass and nettle, mint and dock,
Fill shallow weir, and crumbling lock.

O here upon these banks to stay,
And watch the slow world slide away,
And on this greenness cold and kind
To rest the eyes, to rest the mind.

# EXCESS

Beauty exceeds, too much
For human thought to more than touch,
Human soul to comprehend.
Beauty has no end.
Each leaf of every tree
So beautiful, yet who can see ?
Each song of every bird
So beautiful, yet who has heard
Each of these holy harmonies
That daybreak pours from countless trees ?
No, we must turn to one,
To nightingale who sings alone,
Take in a careful hand
A single flower to understand,
Gaze on, accept, believe
All our senses can perceive,
Truth of hue and scent and touch.
Yet there bloom a million such !
Beauty exceeds, too much.

# CHARLOTTE

Do not go, Branwell,
Away to the Bull —
Stay here with me
Where the air is cool:

Three sisters wait
In the elegant room.
Six eyes watch
For brother to come.

I hold you back
With my delicate hand:
Why do you cry
As if you were burned ?

    'Three burning women
    Pace round the room.
    Flames reach out
    When brother comes home.

    Give me the tavern,
    Give me the grave,
    Spare me the gift
    That my sisters have.'


# THE CLOCK

The wind sat on the steeple,
The bells began to sway:
    'Now tell me all, good people,
    What shall I sweep away ?'

Then loud cried the people,
(The tower began to rock):
    'O leave us the steeple,
    But take away the clock.

    We need not go to work then,
    The hour will never strike;
    We'll never have the time then
    To do what we dislike;

    The night will never come then
    To button up the sky,
    Nor parson call to tell us
    Our time has come to die.'

# DELPHI

Under the olives,
And up the side of the hill,
Where now, Apollo,
Do the white feet linger,
Whence is this music, strayed
Like echo through the rocks ?

The wild thyme is crushed,
And the fragrance rises;
The dark leaves of laurel
Are broken from the way.

The baskets lie empty
About the apple orchard:
The girls are stolen away
To wander after Apollo.
Cropping the roadside grass,
Patient the little donkey waits.

I have seen the storm
Sweep down the holy mountain,
And the dark fierce eagles
Driven shrieking to the plain,
I have seen white columns
Lie shattered about the earth.

   'Go tell the King
   That the walls have fallen,
   The well-built walls are crumbling,
   The stream is dry
   And the sacred laurel withered,
   Mute are the voices,
   And the god gone from his house.'

Long has the sun
Risen in these ruins gleaming,
The olives have grown old
In memory of Apollo.
Grey stand the olives
And green the pines of the hill —
Whence, like a fountain,
Comes this music soaring,
Whither this laughter
That echoes through the woods ?

From the yellow vines
Hang the green grapes thronging.
The gatherers all are gone
To hear the song of Apollo.
The goats unherded climb
The white crags of the mountain;
The cloak and crook forsaken lie.

Someone is singing,
Walking among these hills,
Playing and singing.


# THE IRIS BED


Here, as I lie and wake
To stare against the light,
Birch leaves and catkins break
Clear on my summer sight,
Two strong and separate greens;
Yet when I close my eyes,
Not these, but old lost scenes
    Bewildering rise,

This iris bed, unsought !
Strong stems, green leaves like spears,
Huge purple flowers — my thought
Says, fifty years
Since playground children stayed
To see how brown wet snails
Climbed leaf and stem, and made
    Bright silver trails !

Why should these white walls crack
With sudden purple bloom,
Why stiff green spears hold back
My calm and adult room ?
Great snails, see them crawl
Across these trees and sky !
Do their shining trails recall
    Some inmost I ?

# BEREFT IN MAY

Lay parsley to my wound,
Set campion to my hurt,
Childhood bluebells beautiful
Bind up my heart —
Bluebells, but we took
Our childhood bluebells home;
Where are home and children now ?
What Spring has come ?

Soak up the inward blood
Warm grass and lulling light;
Plenitude of bursting leaves
Crowd through my thought,
Full, strong, careless life
This latter Spring affords,
Hide from me where love has gone
For all my hopes and words.

ISBN 0948478 35 7

Printed by Preseli Printers Ltd., Fishguard, Dyfed.